How to Start Your
Own Business

Tonja Ayers

How To Start Your Own Business

Emperial Publishing

P.O. Box 211194

Detroit, MI 48221-1194

emperialpublishing@gmail.com

www.emperialpublishing.com

Cover Design by 325 Graphics

ISBN: 978-0-557-79400-3

First printing November 2010

Acknowledgements

Thanks Miles Dixon!

How To Start Your Own Business

Table of Contents

How To Start Your Own Business

Who Am I?

My name is Tonja Ayers and I am a Retail Coach. I am an experienced business leader and have been an entrepreneur for 15 years. I have founded several businesses and The Shoe Lady, a women's retail shoe store which opened April 14, 2000 located in Detroit, Michigan has been my greatest success. My years of entrepreneurial experience combined with my training and education enables me to provide you with a wide array of information in the retail arena.

As the founder of The Retail Coach, I have consulted and mentored many independent retailers within the metropolitan Detroit area.

How To Start Your Own Business

In addition to being an entrepreneur and retail guru, I am a published author, fashion writer, artist and wardrobe stylist.

What is Retail?

Retail is the sale of goods in small or individual lots for direct usage by the purchaser. Traditionally, retailing occurred at a fixed location, such as a department store, storefront or kiosk. As of today there are many options in regards to retailing, such as:

- ❑ Storefront
- ❑ Catalog
- ❑ Mail Order
- ❑ Internet
- ❑ Vendoring
- ❑ Home Parties
- ❑ Mall Kiosk

Why Use a Retail Coach?

You can receive many benefits by utilizing a retail coach. A retail coach is similar to an athletic coach. It is the coach's responsibility to coach, train and assist you in obtaining ultimate performance. The following are a few benefits of using a retail coach.

- A retail coach will provide clarity by reviewing your business and marketing plan making it easier to obtain the goals and vision of your organization.

- A retail coach will assist you in determining what needs to be done and how to do it.

- A retail coach will provide encouragement, motivate you and monitor your progress.

- A retail coach will assist in strengthening your leadership skills.

- A retail coach will generate new business ideas and strategies or find ways to modify present policies.

- A retail coach will provide 1-on-1 training.

- A retail coach will become your mentor and business associate.

Do You Have What It Takes?

Many people approach me regarding starting their own businesses. Being self employed is not an easy task. Most say they want to be their own boss however *can* you be your own boss? Do you have what it takes to be your own boss?

Take a few moments to read the following questions? Don't read them one time! Read the questions twice before answering and truly think about what I am asking you.

Read each question and write down your answers.

Do you have a plan? Not just a business plan but a life plan. What are your goals?

_____

_____

_____

_____

Is this the right business for you? Oftentimes, entrepreneurs select businesses that are not "right" for them. Don't select a business because someone else is doing it or because it is the "in" thing. Select something that you are passionate about or have some type of interest in.

Do you have the time, experience and/or resources to commit to this business venture?

After answering each question and carefully reviewing each answer, ask yourself....**Do you have what it takes?**

Are You Ready?

Now that we have determined you have what it takes, there is one more question. Are you ready?

- Is this the right time in your life to start a business?

- Are you willing to sacrifice?

- Do you make good decisions?

- Are you willing to take risks?

- Do you have the ability to lead?

- Do you have experience in management, marketing, accounting and/or sales?

Take a moment to reflect on your strengths and weaknesses.

What are your strengths?

1. _____

2. _____

3. _____

4. _____

5. _____

What are your weaknesses?

1. _____

2. _____

3. _____

4. _____

5. _____

Now that you have determined your strengths and weaknesses you are better equipped for handling certain situations. You are totally aware of what you can and can not do in addition to knowing what you excel in and what areas need reinforcement.

Let's Get Started!

Congratulations! You decided to start your own business. Thousands of Americans decide to start their own businesses every year therefore, you are not alone. However, with that said, competition does exist and you must find your niche. Be creative and innovative when it pertains to the details of your business decisions.

Ready? Set? Let's Get Started!

10 Steps to Starting Your Own

Retail Business

1. Business Structure

2. Business Name

3. Business Registration

4. Select Product

5. Business Plan

6. Location

7. Purchase Inventory

8. Pricing

9. Store Policy

10. Market Business

#1 – Create a Business Structure

Many states, counties and cities have various laws regarding the establishment of business structures. Contact legal assistance or do some research before creating a business entity.

There are advantages and disadvantages to each type of business structure in addition to different tax and legal requirements. The following is a list of common business structures.

❑ Sole Proprietorship

❑ General or Limited
  Partnership

❑ C or S Corporation

❑ Limited Liability Corporation

Types of Business Structures

Sole Proprietorship -- You own the company and are responsible for both its assets and liabilities.

General Partnership -- You contract with one or more people to run the business with equal responsibilities and liabilities.

Limited Partnership -- Some of the partners in the partnership have less interest and liability in the company. In this type of partnership, there must be at least one general partner.

Limited Liability Company -- You structure the company so that you and the people with whom you are starting the company have less or limited liability.

C Corporation -- A traditional corporation that, when set up, leaves you with little or no personal liability.

S Corporation -- The liability aspect is the same as a C corporation. The difference is the way it is taxed. C corporations are taxed twice, once on the corporate level and again on the personal level. S corporations are only taxed on the personal level.

#2 - Choose a Business Name

Although this may appear to be a very easy task, you should put a great deal of thought into naming your business. Your business is your "baby" and you wouldn't name your child the first thing that comes to mind therefore take your time and concentrate on selecting a great and marketable business name.

If you plan on operating as an online business, go to www.pickeepickee.com and check to see if the domain name is available for the business name you have selected.

- Select a name that is easy to spell and pronounce.

- Brainstorm with friends and family.

- Do not select a lengthy name. You want a name that's easy to remember.

- Your name will become your "brand". Select a catchy name that will be easy to brand.

Name Selection Tips

Research your name selection to ensure no negative undertones are associated with the name. For example in 2007, Beaner's coffee was the Midwest's third largest coffee supplier.

Beaner's selected a name to reflect the origin of their product hence the coffee "bean" however the term "beaner" is considered a derogatory slur and deemed offensive by some members of the Hispanic community. Beaner's voluntarily changed their name to Biggby once this concern was brought to management's attention.

How To Start Your Own Business

#3 – Business Registration

Once your business structure has been selected, you will need to register your business entity.

The following steps will need to take place however not necessarily in this order and again depending on the requirements in your region.

- Business Registration – www.irs.gov

- Business Name Registration – Contact your state and city governments for requirements.

- Business Licenses and/or Permits - Contact your state and city governments for requirements.

How To Start Your Own Business

You may need a sales tax license or seller's permit for your area.

#4 - Select Product

I'm quite sure that you have a basic idea of what you would like to sell. You will need to know your product in order to select an accurate business name. Research your product to ensure your selection is something you can commit to wholeheartedly.

If you plan on selling men's suits, do you plan on selling ties and handkerchiefs also? Consider selling merchandise which compliments your primary product line. This process is called vertical integration.

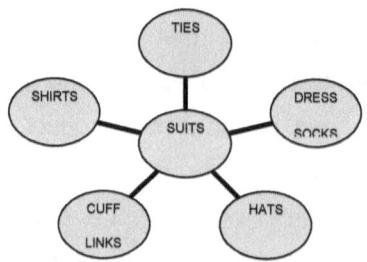

The graph above displays vertical integration in relation to men's suits. The items in the outer circles are complimentary to men's suits. In addition to vertical integration, here are some additional factors to consider when selecting a product.

- Demand – Does anyone want or need what you want to sell?

- Marketability – How difficult will it be to market this product?

- Profit Margin – You control your own profit however you must remember to remain competitive and reasonable when pricing.

- Popularity – Is there a great demand for this product?

- Quality

  - Lesser Quality, Lower Profit Margin

  - Greater Quality, Higher Profit Margin

- Quantity

  - Some vendors offer bulk discounts

Try not to over order especially if there is no great demand for the product.

#5 - Write a Business Plan

If you are looking to acquire funding from a financial institution, you will need a detailed business plan. A business plan helps you put your business into perspective. It forces you to establish goals develop your mission and create a vision.

Most likely you have probably heard the old saying, "businesses fail to plan not plan to fail". Well this statement is very true. A business requires you to develop an exit strategy. Life has many unpredictable twists and turns such as death or divorce. You must be prepared to exit if it becomes necessary to do so.

There are many resources available online where you can receive assistance and download free business plan templates. Try browsing through the following websites for assistance.

❑ Score www.score.org

❑ Small Business
   Administration www.sba.gov

#6 – Location

Where do you plan on conducting business?

- ❑ Mall

- ❑ Kiosk

- ❑ Storefront

- ❑ Flea Market

- ❑ Website

- ❑ Vendoring

- ❑ Catalog

How much space do you need? Ordinarily your lease amount will be determined by the amount of space you need to rent. A person selling bicycles would need more space than a person selling handbags. Be sure to consider product size and the amount of inventory you plan on maintaining at one time in addition to the following items.

- How much rent can you afford?
- Check with your city government to determine if your location selection is zoned for retail.
- The physical appearance of the location AND its surrounding area.
- Lighting
- Parking
- Handicap accessibility
- Visibility
- Does your target market frequent this area?
- Competition in the area

Storefront Design

Store design is a very important aspect of your retail operation. The store design creates a certain atmosphere and sometimes simply the appearance of your store will draw a customer in. Atmosphere will also determine if a customer will become a reoccurring customer. Store design is a component of the shopping experience.

Start from the outside. The outside is what the customer sees first. Stand outside and look inside. What do you see? Do you like what you see? Would you want to shop there?

People often say don't judge a book by its cover however most people do the exact opposite and in some cases it's

37

the cover that actually sells the book.
IMAGE IS EVERYTHING!

Storefront Do's & Don'ts

- Do greet customers upon their arrival. When a customer enters your establishment, acknowledge their presence by greeting them and inquiring if they are in need of any assistance.

- Do have adequate lighting. A dark and dismal store may create a depressive atmosphere and therefore discourage customers from shopping.

- Do have your thermostat set at a comfortable temperature. Try to have your store cool during the summer months and warm during the winter months. Customers will not stay if the temperature is uncomfortable.

- Do keep display areas neat and tidy.

Location/Storefront Tips

These are a few items to consider:

- Wall colors & decorations

- Background music & sounds

- Ergonomics – Try not to place inventory too low or too high

- Avoid clutter & narrow aisle ways

- Aroma – avoid strong fragrances

- Eye candy – window display should be appealing

- Cleanliness – Store should be free of dust, debris and dirt.

#7 – Purchase Inventory

- Who will you purchase from?

    - Wholesalers

        - First runs

        - Closeouts/Liquidations

    - Manufacturers

    - Importers

    - Auctioneers

- Where and how will you make purchases?

    - Tradeshows

    - Internet

    - Catalogs

    - Retail Buyer

42

- Be creative! Think outside the box

  - Local artists – You may want to consider selling the work of local designers, painters, jewelry makers, etc on a consignment basis.

  - Public auctions – Check your local newspaper for public auctions. This is a great way to obtain bulk inventory and store fixtures.

  - Storage units – Most storage facilities hold a monthly auction for unpaid storage units.

  - Craigslist, EBay, etc. – Businesses utilize these

types   of   sites   when
liquidating their assets.

Tradeshows

Trade shows provide an excellent means of remaining competitive. Many wholesalers base future products on responses and reactions of trade show attendees. Be the first to order or sell a particular item in your area by placing orders at trade shows. By attending trade shows you will be able to meet sales representatives and even actual owners of various companies face-to-face therefore building a rapport with the organization.

Trade shows can become overwhelming however with proper planning and organization you can obtain all of your goals and meet some that you never even knew you had!

Establish a budget. Determine how much you plan on spending and what you plan on spending it on. Do you plan on spending $10,000 on footwear and $5,000 on handbags? Set a limit and stick to it!

- Identify the needs of your organization. What needs to be ordered? Have an idea of what to look for and be sure to only purchase the necessities. If your budget allows extra spending, only do so after all of the necessities have been acquired.

- Make a list of vendors that you would like to see and make appointments if possible.

- Do your research? Is this the right show for you? If you have a shoe store and only sell shoes and/or shoe related products, you may not want to attend a trade show that exhibits primarily clothing.

- Pre-Register! By pre-registering you will save time and avoid long registration lines.

- Many trade shows offer workshops and seminars relating to the retail industry. Do some research and reserve a seat at a class or two if your schedule permits.

- Image is everything! You are representing your business. Your dress code should be business

47

casual and be sure to wear comfortable shoes.

- Bring plenty of business cards. Always have pen and paper.

- Many trade shows provide free gifts and samples. Be prepared to ship them back to your store or save space in your suitcase for catalogs, gift bags, etc.

- Most trade shows have some type of discount arrangement made with a nearby hotel for show attendees. Be sure to check with trade show coordinators to save money on lodging expenses.

- By following my trade show tips, I am quite sure that you will have a great time, make new contacts and have a wonderful shopping experience.

Capital

You have an idea of who you are going to order from and what you are going to order. Now you need to determine how are you going to pay for your inventory?

- ❑ Cash

  - ■ Savings

  - ■ Investors

  - ■ Family & Friends

- ❑ Terms

- ❑ Credit Lines

- ❑ Retirement

- ❑ Piggy Bank

Capital Raising Tips

1. Make sure that you have a good business plan. Potential investors will want to see your goals, objectives and financial projections.

2. Ask for "enough" money! Many businesses fail because they started without enough money. You will need to have a cushion for expected expenditures and slow sales.

3. Try not to have too many investors. Everyone needs to be on the same page when it comes to goals and objectives of the business. It is more difficult to get

10 people to agree on something than it is 2 people.

4. Investor agreements need to be detailed and thorough. Investors need to know when and how much they will be paid.

#8 - Pricing

Pricing Strategy

- Multiples – You may want to offer a discount if multiple items are purchased. For example, "Buy 4 Get 1 Free!"

- Psychological – You may want to price items with .95 cents or .99 cents endings.

Markup

- Cost of Goods + Markup = Retail Price

- Determine your markup percentage

  - 200%, 500%, 700%

53

- Would you purchase this particular item for this price?

- What is the affordability of your target market?

- Be Competitive – Check out the competition to ensure your prices are competitive.

- Consider the cost and operating expenses associated with the product when pricing.

Store Policy

You must establish store policies to ensure day to day operations run smoothly.

- Define Hours & Days of Operation
    - Create Work Schedule
- Types of Payments
    - Cash
    - Credit/Debit
    - Check
    - Installments/Layaway
- Returns
    - Will you accept returns or establish a final sale policy?

- o If you decide to accept returns, will you enforce a timeline? 7 days? 14 days?

- o With or without a receipt?

- Exchanges

- Store Credit

- Refunds

Work Schedule

Creating a work schedule is one of the most important aspects of the daily operations in a retail business. Being understaffed may cause customers to become irate due to the wait, you may lose revenue due to those customers who become impatient and decide to leave or those who consider this to be a bad shopping experience and decide not to return. Not to mention the word of mouth factor. Previous customers may give a negative review to their peers or not suggest your place of business due to a less than satisfactory shopping experience.

Things to Consider When Scheduling

- **Peak Sales Periods** – Analyze your peak sales hours in order to determine how many staff members need to be staffed for that particular timeframe. You want to ensure adequate manpower during peak times of the day and/or days of the week. For example, if you have a candy store across the street from a high school, you may need an extra sales clerk during lunch hour and after school. However, during the summer months when school is not in session, you may need not to schedule additional help.

- **Size of Store** – If you have a large store, you may need to schedule additional employee(s) to provide better customer service to your customers. Your customers should not have to search for a salesperson to obtain assistance.

- **Holidays/Sales/Special Events** – Try to be mindful of upcoming holidays and events when creating a schedule. It's almost impossible to forget about Christmas but stay aware of other holidays which may create additional foot traffic for you or a neighboring business. For example, you have a jewelry store and you do pretty well with Valentine's Day sales. However, the Italian restaurant next door to your store is having a $19.99 Valentine's Day dinner special for couples. You might want to consider staying open later to accommodate dinner guests who are waiting for a table or walking past your storefront.

- Overstaffing is also an issue. You do not want to have idle salespersons. Idle sales people equal loss revenue.

Market Business

Marketing is the process utilized to create interest in your product or service. A marketing plan details the actions required to achieve your marketing objectives.

First and most importantly, one needs to determine their target market. Who will you sell to?

- o Gender
- o Age
- o Income
- o Race

Why is your target market so important? Because your target market defines the **basis** of your business.

o Your business name should be *based* on your target market. If selling kids shoes, your name should reflect that.

o Your suppliers and your price points are *based* on your target market.

o Style selections are *based* on your target market. If your market is women over 60, you wouldn't stock your store with mini skirts.

Always consider your market when purchasing inventory and continuously analyze your target market. After opening, you may notice a different demand versus what you originally anticipated. I have a business associate who decided to open a candy store across the street from a high school. Her sales were mediocre however one day she had eaten pizza prior to some of the students entering her store and they all mentioned how they were hungry and how good the pizza smelled. She decided to purchase a few pizzas and sell slices to the students. Well this idea was great however she later discovered this was illegal because her store was not zoned or licensed to sell food. She decided to make the big leap and apply for food licensing and permits after she found a deal on a pizza oven on Craigslist. She made her investment on the permits and machinery back in less than 90 days. This was a brave and strategic move but also an excellent example of how one must analyze their market.

Second, how do you plan to market your business?

- o Radio/Television Advertisements

- o Print Ads

- o Newspapers, Magazines

- o Billboards

- o Flyers, Brochures, Postcards

- o Internet

  - Ads

  - Website

  - Blogs

  - Banner Sharing

- Social Media Networks

  - Facebook

  - Twitter

  - MySpace

  - LinkedIn

There are several benefits of utilizing social media networks.

- It's FREE

- Increases your search result ranking therefore creating more exposure for your business

- Serves as a broadcast tool

- Allows you to build your brand

- You posses the ability to create a "buzz" about your product

How Are You Going to Sell?

How do you plan on selling your goods? What is your "process"?

- How do you plan on selling your product to the people?

- What marketing techniques will you use? For example, I maintain a text list for my shoe store at www.eztexting.com. When a new shoe arrives, all customers who have subscribed to the text list will receive a message and picture of the new arrival.

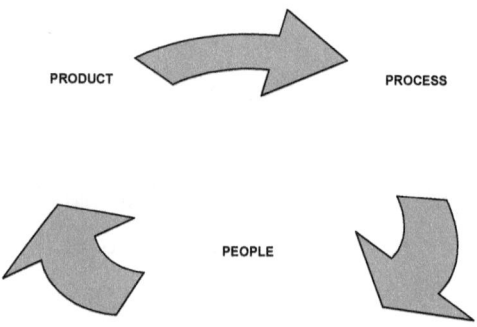

PRODUCT   PROCESS

PEOPLE

How do you plan on getting your product or word about your product to the people?

TIPS

Customer Service

- Answer door and/or greet customer promptly.

- Be punctual. Store should be open during posted store hours.

- Be helpful but not overbearing.

- Avoid personal phone calls and texting in the presence of customers.

- Ask questions and be open to suggestions.

- Customers have options. They chose to shop with you therefore treat them accordingly.

Public Relations

- Maintain relationships within the community. Interact with community based associations and organizations.

Insurance

Contact several insurance agencies to request quotes for insurance. You will need to know what you want to insure and for how much? Also consider what type of insurance you will need. If your business is located near or around a possible flood zone you may want to add flood insurance.

- Options:

    - Fire

    - Theft

❑ Flood

❑ Liability

❑ Auto, if you use your auto for your business.

Security

Although we may want to think that we live in a perfect and crime free world…we don't. You will need to implement some type of security system for your investment.

There are many options to choose from:

❑ Alarm

❑ Security Guard

❑ Surveillance System

■ Indoor and/or outdoor

Mentor

Find a mentor with experience in your retail area. A mentor can share their entrepreneurial experience. The following are a few benefits of having a mentor.

- Experience

- Wisdom

- Guidance

- Networking – A mentor can offer you access to their extended network.

Join retail related associations to stay abreast of trends, market forecasts, tradeshows and upcoming events with your specific industry.

- ❑ National Retail Federation – www.nrf.com

- ❑ Retail Industry Leaders Association – www.rila.org

- ❑ United Shoe Retailers Association – www.usraonline.org

- ❑ National Shoe Retailers Organization – www.nsra.org

- ❑ American Apparel & Footwear Organization – www.americanapparel.org

Ok! Now you know the 10 steps to starting your own business. To be honest, getting started is the easy part. Anyone can open a business, but it takes great discipline and creativity to master obtaining new customers. Learn to become a critical thinker.

I appreciate you giving me an opportunity to "coach" you in regards to starting your own business. Good luck and I wish you much success with your business endeavors!

NEED HELP?

If you need additional assistance, I provide the following services.

- Retail Buyer

  - ❑ Merchandise Selection

  - ❑ Product Forecasting

- Retail Consulting

  - ❑ Retail Strategy Creation

  - ❑ Concept Development

  - ❑ Strategy Implementation

- Retail Training

  - ❑ Customer Service

  - ❑ Sales

- Retail Marketing

How To Start Your Own Business

- ❑ Database Building

- ❑ Social Media Marketing

- ❑ Sales Promotions

- ❑ Public Relations

- ❑ Branding

- ❑ Advertising

My services are based upon the various requests I receive however they are not limited to the services listed above. If you have a question please feel free to inquire.

Give me a call! I'm here if you need me!

(313) 444-4BIZ

tonja@theretailcoach.biz

www.theretailcoach.biz

THE RETAIL COACH